SEA GLASS

POEMS

by

JIM MENGERT

COVER ART BY LAURA NALESNIK

TYPOGRAPHICAL DESIGN BY
GREG HUGHES OF CRANE METAMARKETING LTD.

TITLE BY JIM HINSON

CONTENTS

Foreword   vii

Once   1

Timing is Everything   2

La vie en rose   3

Intimations of Mortality   4

The Word   5

A Boy   6

Champ   7

Pietà   8

The Old Prayers   9

Sea Turtle   10

Threshold   11

Secret   12

Winter Trees   13

Anniversary   14

What Have They Done With My Lord?   15

"With how sad steps, O moon, thou climb'st the skies"   16

The Leaf Blower   17

The Dead   18

Ah   19

Just Desert   20

Storyteller   21

Ginkgo Biloba in the Fall   22

Your Messages on the Answering Machine   23

History   24

Performing for Company   25

Little Sister   26

New Year's Eve, 2008   27

Next in Line   28

Afterlife   29

Genesis   30

...and there was light   31

Prometheus   32

Azaleas   33

Old Men   34

CONTENTS

Same Difference	35
Out of His Element	36
Two Little Boys	37
The Question	38
Paul	39
"Leave Me, O Love"	40
Better Late Than Never	41
Ann Cobb	42
Baseball Season	43
Lightning Bugs	44
Missing	45
Between Rounds	46
"Che gelida manina" 1964	47
Memory	48
Horace	49
Yes	50
Curtain	51
"Memory may be beautiful, and yet..."	52
Palliative Care	53
Spring	54
Maybe This Time	55
Brief Candle	56
Allergy	57
Summer Now and Then	58
Her Laugh	59
Protest	60
The Lover's Excuse	61
Tiktaalik: Or, In the Beginning	62
Exodus	63
Ashes in a Cookie Tin	64
Hearthstone	65
Neighbor	66
Navel	67
Fill in the Blanks	68

CONTENTS

Auto Biography	69
Tweaking Charlotte	70
Good Friday	71
Steak Dinner	72
Remembering...	73
Just Friends	74
"And the great shroud of the sea rolled on..."	75
Sea Glass	76
Gardenia	77
"Cosi Fan Tutte"	78
Romeo	79
Dave	80
Got to	81
Us	82
All Hallows	83
The Grudge	84
Fishing	85
Regret	86
Break Up	87
Untitled	88
Disfavor	89
Dog Walking	90
Water Works	91
The Readiness is All	92
Retaining Wall	93
My Tribe	94
Making the Team	95
Revival	96
Wrath	97
A Fish Story	98
Non-Canonical Hour	99
Cantemus	100
Index of Titles	103
About the Author	109

FOREWORD

For more than a decade I have been sending copies
of my poems to several friends. Over time, as the
number of poems grew, many of these friends
urged me to collect them—first for their own benefit,
because they wanted a format more convenient
than a bulging electronic or paper file; and second,
for the benefit of others because, they believed,
my poems deserved a wider audience.

So this little book exists because of their
encouragement, and I hope that they will
accept it as the best expression of my gratitude
and thanks.

And I also hope that these poems will find new
readers, who will of course decide for themselves
whether my friends' encouragement was evidence
more of deep affection than good judgment. At the
least I am confident that, in reading them, they
will recognize a kindred spirit, someone for whom
poetry is not only an abiding pleasure, but also
an indispensable resource for understanding
and expanding our experience of life.

ONCE

I love once.

Not just because
Once is rabbit hole down, wormhole through and portal to
The wonders of once upon a time.

I love once
Because it pulls a train of consequences.
This once known, that once done,
Then
The plot begins to run.

I love once
Because it marks the threshold,
The once in a lifetime unrepeatable,
The forever
And never again.

Most of all,
I love once
Because once
I loved.

TIMING IS EVERYTHING

It's certainly more dramatic,
More fit for stage or screen,
To reveal some juicy secret
In the final scene—
To let it out
With your expiring breath
And pass disburdened
Through the door
Of death.

But it usually happens
Otherwise.
Secrets tumble out
When you begin to feel like
History,
All interested parties absent
In body or in mind.
New rules apply,
And no exposure is indecent
That brings you back again
To life.

LA VIE EN ROSE

To have had it, even once—
the disregarding passion
that carries you across the threshold
limp in unaccustomed arms—
is to remember, when the ribbon of time
unspools in a tedious line,
that once it went round and round,
whirled and twirled and wound
into a bow on the gift
of almost
everything.

are not like tinnitus, though disabling for some
and strenuously ignored by others,
but more like the tick of the clock
inside the crocodile
pursuing Captain Hook:
a soundless background of anxious anticipation
punctuated
by an occasional five-alarm panic.

The panic actually helps.
It focuses the fear,
gives it a local habitation and a name,
a fire to put out,
a clear escape route.

Smee asked the important question:
What happens when the clock in the croc
runs down?
Hook didn't answer, but Hamlet did:
The rest is silence.

THE WORD

It came uncalled for,
Not one of those words
You rehearse in your head
But leave forever unsaid,
Or a word you save
Like the good china
For a special occasion:
But from a different discourse,
Out of its natural habitat.
Yet it slipped easily from my lips
As if headed for home and
Sure of its welcome
From the first man I ever loved.
Sitting by the bed,
Watching that mighty life ebb relentlessly away,
I heard myself say
Sweetheart
To my father.

A BOY

Alone in the woods
On an after school afternoon
In a pine straw strewn world
All his own,
Something in the deepening shade
Arouses abandon:
He runs naked as native
To the place,
Letting the soft air touch him
Everywhere.
He runs, jumps, swings
From low branches.
And he dances,
Dances in a dream of
Self delight:
Alive, alone,
Until the bugle blast for dinner
Calls him home.

CHAMP

Was there applause and acclamation?
Did your razzle dazzle them?
Was your comeback all
It needed to be
A comeback?

Once more you're the cynosure
Of all beholding,
King of the hill,
Top of the heap.
You still have what it takes
To take their breath away.

But you've been here before.
You know that beneath these waves
Of admiration
Runs a rip tide of expectation,
Taking you out,
Making you outdo yourself
Over and over
And over
Again.

PIETÀ

Hammer and chisel
Have fixed your gaze
Forever
On his body laid
So long across your lap,
Cooled into marble.
No deposition from your cross:
This is your kingdom come.

Once before you held him
Naked,
Wrapped him then in swaddling clothes,
Laid him in the manger.
Now you cannot reach to the winding sheet,
Or rise
To lay him in the tomb.

What creator's pride could dare
To petrify you so,
To polish your helplessness to such a sheen?
How could he bear to make your grief
So everlastingly
Beautiful?

THE OLD PRAYERS

They were night light and launching pad,
Soft lap and suit of armor.
They were neighbors next door
And rich relations far away.

They were spells to raise
Beneficent powers
And consolation in the midnight
Hours.

But only one prayer prays now
As it did then:
On the threshold of silence
The acquiescent Amen.

SEA TURTLE

What if we two should meet tonight,
You and I,
While the half moon makes the ocean brighter
Than the sky:
You, of that ancient mariner line
Familiar in the deepest seas
When dinosaurs were novelties;
I, though only yards from home,
A little lost, a lot
Alone.

How many years and ocean miles rewind
Until the breaking water births you back
To this same shore where you began
To begin again,
Toiling up the beach to find
Refuge for the future of your kind.

Come tonight. Let me witness your
Immemorial mystery.
Shower me with the sand
You scatter and gather again
So carefully.
Maybe then, when you return
To the safety of the sea,
You will leave new life nesting
Even in me.

THRESHOLD

Precariously poised
On the rim of a flower pot,
A bird new fledged looked out
At the brave new world before him:
The expanse of buoying air
—And possible perches everywhere.

He clung almost immobile
Between earth and sky,
As if deciding whether, when,
Or where to fly.

Or remembering if still he could
The cluster of the nest,
The freighted beak,
The covering breast.

SECRET

The secret shackled you
To a diminished self.
Yet you layered your life
Around it.
It was your difference.
If they only knew.

Your shame became your treasure,
And hiding hoarding:
Stigmata of the spirit,
A glorious wound, a wounded glory.

Eventually
You couldn't even tell
What you were afraid of—
The discovery or
The loss.

WINTER TREES

Trees without leaves
Are not ashamed
To be displayed
So unarrayed.
Their bared limbs lifted high
Scratch winter's name
Into the sky,
Uncensored,
Unadorned.

They expose themselves
To our inspection,
Without embarrassment:
Altitude with attitude.

And rightly so.
For theirs is not a strip that teases.
It delivers.
What summer finery obscures
Their winter peel reveals,
Allowing us to see
How comely the scaffolding of life
Can be.

ANNIVERSARY

Today I've known you
For as long
As I didn't:
Dividing into equal parts
The ardent and the arduous
Years.
Tomorrow I'll know us more
Than all the years
Before.

WHAT HAVE THEY DONE WITH MY LORD?

Somebody's been stealing Jesus.
All over town
Nativity scenes are turning into
Crime scenes.

Stolid Joseph and postpartum Mary
Don't seem to notice.
They hover dutifully over the empty manger,
Witnessing divine transcendence.

The Angel with her Rockette face
And beauty queen banner
Keeps belting out Glorias
Oblivious to the absence of the Star.

If the shepherds feel duped
Into their midnight hike
For this spectacular
Non Event
They aren't showing it.

And the animals seem quite content
That someone had the good sense
To get that baby out
Of their food supply.

The surprise is that anyone noticed.
After all,
Taking Christ out of Christmas
Is hardly news.
Expressions of concern are no doubt sincere
And deeply felt.
No one likes to break up a set.

"WITH HOW SAD STEPS, O MOON, THOU CLIMB'ST THE SKIES"

The moon, they say, is moving away,
But at a decorous pace,
Befitting a lady of illustrious line
Once considered divine.
Long before her faintest glimmer fails,
Lovers will have switched allegiance to the stars
And tides forgot how once they took the beaches
Without storm.
She will not witness our ultimate demise,
When the sun at last burns black:
Which on reflection seems the only proper way,
That the night light should go out
Before the day.

THE LEAF BLOWER

He harries the leaves
With more roar
Than the winds that tore them
From the trees
Churning in dust and air.

No stragglers are allowed.
Even one left leaf
Offends.
And the task ends only
When all of fall is bagged
Or blown away.

Me, I'd rather rake than blow.
Raking is a rhythm,
Not a roar:
Reaching out and gathering in,
Not driving all before.
Untidy, it leaves leaves
Behind, as if to remind
That fall was, and perfect
Will never be.

THE DEAD

The longer they're gone
The closer they get.
They turn up everywhere:
On a postcard stuck in an old book,
In a favorite expression dropped
Into a stranger's conversation,
In the sound of a son's voice
Or a daughter's laugh,
Or your own face glimpsed
In a store window.
And they're always lurking
In the Christmas decorations.

They enter your dreams
Without a by your leave
And leave without a goodbye.
You can't shake them
However much you try.
They are shadows
Stitched to your back.

This is their afterlife.
Is it any wonder
That they live it to the full—
Knowing as they do
That they must die again,
With you.

AH

Each an ah:
The grape green red or black
Crushed against the palate fine,
That first delicious surrender
To the splendor in the grass,
And the grasp of something suddenly
Understood.

The last breath as it goes
Will recapitulate all those,
Each remembered ah stretched
Into one last hurrah
For life.

JUST DESERT

What poison poured into your ear
Makes it so hard for you to hear a
Compliment?
Why does it seem unseemly
To accept the due of your
Devotion?
Why must you parry every word of
Praise?

Always in the confession line,
Examining your conscience,
Fingering your faults like rosary beads,
Sure that the postern gate is your only way
To heaven—

When a triumphal entry is your just desert:
With angels clapping wings in loud applause,
With trumpet blast and alleluia cry,
And halos, flung like frisbees, shimmering
In the sky.

STORYTELLER

Even in those black shoes
That nuns used to wear
Your feet from the wide swing
Couldn't reach the ground,
And around your neck
Hung a hearing aid huge
As a pectoral cross
And always of uncertain
Operation.

But your ears were tuned to other voices:
The wide swing under summer shade
You made into a magic carpet,
Sweetening the ride with butterscotch candy.
Poverty had enriched your imagination
And your eyes black as the coal
You once changed your religion for
Saw things invisible to mortal sight.

O Grandmother,
Once upon a time
Never seemed so true
As on that summer swing
With you.

GINKGO BILOBA IN THE FALL

This most ancient of our trees
Evolved a rare community of leaves:
They collaborate their collapse
And as they go
Make the season's loveliest show.

First they drain through every vein
Their summer green
And fill with buttery gold
The in between,
Until at last they blaze into a dome
Of monochrome.

Then in just a single day
They fall or blow away.

This precipitous unanimous demise
Reveals the wild disorder of the limbs—
Like flailing gestures of despair
For being left so suddenly
Bare.

YOUR MESSAGES ON THE ANSWERING MACHINE

They would be my harvest,
My hoard in the lean time,
Salt for my table,
Oil for my lamp,
Salve for the sting
Of memory.

I saved them one by one,
A request, a reminder,
A reminiscence.
Not always answering the ring
Just to add another to the string—

But when the day came,
That day stocked up and stored for,
The earth tipped so far into the dark
I couldn't see to press PLAY.

HISTORY
ACCORDING TO A SECOND CHILD

Primogeniture has its privileges:
Titles, inheritances,
New clothes.
God is only God because
He was here first.

Still,
That first first-born must have been
Quite a surprise.
The original wunderkind.
How did we do it?
What do we do with it?
They could have eaten it,
Or traded it for a soft fur.
Instead they saw potential
And decided to try again—
No doubt hoping even then
For a new and better version.

When did you figure it out?
When did you realize
that their applause was laced with
mockery?
How many parties did it take?
How many entries into the arena
of adult approbation
before you finally said no?

It wasn't the words.
You knew the words
to "April Love"
as well as Pat Boone himself.
No, it was the tune.
The tune was just too much
for you to carry.
We knew. Everyone knew.
When did you?

O, little brother, you learned much earlier than I
the perils of performance.
Your tin ear saved you from that siren song:
No long foundering for you,
just a brief fling, like April love.

LITTLE SISTER

It is long enough ago
To be almost once upon a time,
When sex was winks and whispers
In a thicket of dirty words.
It was magazines in brown bags
Bought in a seedy shop
By the bus station,
And furtive solitary pleasure
Risking blindness and the wrath
Of God.

Then mother's belly swelled
And she let me feel her life
And yours.
I watched you both
Grow and grow
Until
Early one midsummer morn,
Like the simple answer to
A complicated question,
You were born.

NEW YEAR'S EVE, 2008

The sun just hung,
Refusing to drop,
A great blazing blot
Over a landscape
Tired of waiting:
For Godsake set, I cried,
And let me cheer the end
Of this calamitous year!
Still it clung,
Stubbornly,
As if any light
Were better
Than the night.

NEXT IN LINE

The man ahead of me
in the checkout line
was taking a very long time
to pay. Again and again
he tried to slide his card
along the groove
and push the button
to approve the transaction:
repeating and repeating,
because the tremor in his hands
kept defeating him.

Murmurs began behind me.
The cashier offered help.
I only stood and watched
and waited.

Soon enough
his place in the line
will be mine.

AFTERLIFE

The diagnosis comes down
Swift and sharp as the blade
Of the guillotine.
Stunned, stupid, disbelieving,
I sit with my head
In my hands.

Outside, in the street, in the crowd,
I am alien, apart.
Surely they can see it:
That man with his head
In his hands.

I try to be who I was
By doing what I did,
The familiar things.
But nothing's the same
When you're holding your head
In your hands.

GENESIS

Being neither first born nor sui generis
I live on hand me downs—
The erstwhile pleasures and the certified treasures
Of those going or gone before.

Big at first for growing into,
Ever tighter over time,
They are outer skin to me,
Inner bone,
Homage and bondage
To home.

But within this encumbering self
Some residue of me
Insists on imagining
What new would be.

The morning sun lays gold on green,
On glass, on ground. It spills down
Walls and flows on floors
Carpeted and bare.

It burnishes the brass
Corners of the campaign chest
And turns its fine craze into
Veins of ore.

Things dulled by the dark
Seem in this light
New
And richly dight.

Such prodigality of celestial treasure
Stirs an ancient urge
To worship:
With lifted arms and open palms
To praise the power that makes
Each day this ordinary
Glory.

PROMETHEUS

If the myth were true
That we owe ourselves to you,
We would be kinder to our kind
And more careful keepers
Of the earth.
If foresight had fathered us,
We would not be this myopic
Misnomered homo sapiens
Living for the profit or the pleasure
Of a day.

If not our creator then, be our redeemer:
Take back your fire.
Bring down the dark.
Make us start again
So that we might be,
If not too wise, at least
Too weak to do harm.

AZALEAS

They were warming up for their proud flourish
Of pink and purple, red and white.
Then came the frost, and in one night
Undid a year's preparation,
A crescendo of expectation.
The blast from Canada muted the blast
Meant to be theirs,
The brass section of the spring.

Still, they sound what notes they can,
Pushing petals apart to blow,
Diminuendo, though,
For spring, like pride,
Always goes before
A fall.

OLD MEN

Eventually
You begin to notice
That old men look more
Like each other
Than themselves:
Circle enough around the sun
And layers of individuation
Come undone,
Exposing family resemblances.
Still-growing ears and noses,
Like tree rings, register the years,
And all the lines read the same,
Whatever the language
Or the name.
They finish at the starting gate,
Where their race began,
Undistinguished members of the brotherhood
Of man.

SAME DIFFERENCE

Sweat-basted
My skinny body sticks
To the yellow aluminum patio chair
While Ricky Nelson goes down to Lonesome Town
And the blaze of noon scatters
The heavenly shades of night falling
On the Platters' Twilight Time.

All for a tan:
A boy awkward and ambivalent
Soliciting the sun
To color him acceptable
So he can hide in its shade.

No music now,
Except the ringing in my ear.
But I am here
In the same chair
Exposing skin I'm still
Not comfortable in
To the alchemy of the same sun.

But different:
Then I sat as long as I could stand
To get a tan
For others to see.
Now it's careful calibration:
Just enough for vitamin D.

OUT OF HIS ELEMENT

The polar vortex wobbled down
To South Dakota
And to a young man up
From Georgia
Unaware
How quick frost bites
In bitter air.

So
When his truck stuck in snow
He didn't know the choice
Was life or limb:
Mere minutes outside
Saved his ride but not
His walk,
Not on those feet,
Not ever again.

The vortex steadied
Round its arctic home,
Leaving him unsteady,
With a wobble all his own.

TWO LITTLE BOYS

I saw them dash
Through the bushes and
Across the grass—
Two little boys so similar
In shape and size
The one behind seemed
Déjà vu.

Round and round the yard they raced
Until I couldn't tell the chaser
From the chased—
Like painted figures on an urn
Now pursuing, now pursued, depending
On the turn.

I left them there, stretching
Their summer growth of limb
In the crisp fall air,
Running into their lives.

THE QUESTION

Now I'm old. You're dead.
But still the scene plays in my head:
Me at my desk doing homework,
You suddenly towering there,
Fumbling toward your question.

I was just a kid,
Sure only of my shame,
Steeped in fear.
So I told you
What you wanted to hear.

You had wrestled your revulsion
And chosen love—
Braver far than I,
Who in that moment faltered
And chose the lie.

In all the years since then
You never asked again.

PAUL

Like beads on a string
They mark the old man's wandering:
Antioch on the Orontes,
Pessinus. Ephesus. Philippi. Thessalonika.
Corinth.
Rome.
An unlikely Odysseus, he moved ever
Toward the beckoning west,
Trying to get to the world's end
Before it ended.

He was a difficult man,
Wearing out his welcome as often
As his shoes.
A ridiculous man,
Sowing seeds in cities,
Expecting others to cultivate them.

It began as an ordinary trip
Between two particular cities,
One to leave from, one to arrive at,
And the road was just a road.
But somewhere between
The road became the Way,
And no city could hold him after.

Itinerant, indefatigable,
He kept himself moving
Along other roads,
Certain that somewhere
Between two other cities
It would happen again.

"LEAVE ME, O LOVE"

After his infarction,
The prescription was
A smaller dose of me—
Because, apparently,
I am too weak
To steady Jacob's ladder.

His circle contracted and left me
In the we'll call you world,
My presence no longer a must,
My love numbered with those
That reach but to dust.

His aspiration is the aperture
Beyond the highest rung.
So he keeps on contracting,
Hoping that the final one
Will push him through.

BETTER LATE THAN NEVER

Each day another memory
slips away. More and more
her eyes see things
she doesn't know.

But she still knows me,
and in this melting of her mind
I find an unexpected grace: a flood
of praise and love and gratefulness.
I stand in the shower of her words,
so warm, so waited for:
bright, brief flowers on a forest floor,
between winter's freeze and shadowing leaves.

The bed next to my mother's was empty today.
She's gone down to the dementia ward,
One floor below.

Mrs. Cobb, I hardly knew you.
I knew of a fall and an operation.
I knew of a son and daughter,
Though not by name,
Because they never came.
I heard a voice, a Southern voice, a Lady voice,
Polite in pain.
Please. Please don't hurt me.
I saw a smile, a sudden smile,
The bravery of a retreating mind,
That lighted once a lovely mile.

The bed next to my mother's was empty today.
She's gone down to the dementia ward,
One floor below.

BASEBALL SEASON

Baseball reminds us that
Even spring needs
Training:
After winter's stiffening grip,
Even the natural can't perform
Without a warm up to the
Opening day.
Otherwise, what chance for
The perfect rose?

LIGHTNING BUGS

Lightning bugs abounded once,
Enough to catch in your hands
And collect in a jar.
They were the decoration
Of a summer night,
Each one a twinkling terrestrial
Star.

I saw two tonight,
Or one twice, and wondered
Where they all have gone:
Migrated to a more
Hospitable clime or
Joined the long forced march
To extinction.

Perhaps they still festoon
The night, flash and flicker
In the summer air—and it's just my
Diminished sight
That makes them seem so
Rare.

MISSING

Missing.
Gone missing we say, as if missing
Were fishing,
As if they chose,
Even if they took no gear,
Packed no clothes.

Missing,
Missing in action we say, as if missing
Were not inaction,
As if they still fight
Translated to some other sphere
Out of sight.

Missing.
Missing you, we say, as if missing
Were misplacing,
As if you were somewhere around,
Needing only a thorough search
To be found.

But
Missing is a stake in the heart
That impertinently persists
Without missing
A beat.

BETWEEN ROUNDS

Even sadness has to rest,
To discompose those features too familiar.
To release that hold squeezed all the way to
Numb.

But you can't plan for it:
A surprise slant of sun
Through clouds collecting dusk;
Your favorite song falling
From an open window;
The flat surface of your mind
Suddenly rippling
Your mother's smile.

You are refreshed.
And so is he.

"CHE GELIDA MANINA" 1964

He hit *hope* on the high note
And we were one in wonder.
I imagined then an impossible hunger
Satisfied: your hand
Like hers in his in mine.
O, speranza! Pitch perfect leap
Into Lethe and
I didn't know I knew
The story's end.

MEMORY

Memory is lubricious,
Notoriously capricious;
It embroiders the delicious,
Annuls the vicious,
And ignores the everydays
That enrich us.

It exaggerates,
Manipulates,
Cuts and pastes
And profligately wastes
Most of the material
It has to work with.

But you've got to trust it,
However false or true,
Because without it
There isn't any you.

HORACE

Companion of short winter days,
Accept in this language not your own
My words of thanks and praise.

No priest now climbs the Capitol,
No vestals nurse the sacred flame,
Imperial glories like the Sibyl's leaves
Are scattered in the wind.

But the monument you made
Of ordinary life laid out
In intricate and elegant designs
Shines still: more enduring than brass
And, yes, higher than star-pointing pyramids.
All of you has not died:
Thanks to your better part
Your dead language speaks again
And warms this winter heart.

YES

Yes is so easy to say.
Almost slackadaisical:
The jaw drops, and the mouth exhales
Its soothing sibilance.

The caress of yes makes babies and
True believers.
Assent is something you just fall into,
Like bad company or
Easy virtue.

But why in that sibilant sigh
Do I hear the hiss of
Subservience,
Recognize
In that easy letting go of breath
The sweat of my brow and
The shadow of death?

Nothing is so easy as yes
To say,
But no is safer far for
Every day.

CURTAIN

Hands that applauded before
Now direct you toward the door.
The party's over for you
Who once were the life of it.

So you're passed your prime.
So sometimes your stride slips,
You fumble a line,
Or drop a name.

But why this bum's rush?

No matter. Here's the door.
Shake off their hands.
Straighten up.
Survey the scene with expert eye
And, remembering who you are,
Exit like a star.

"MEMORY MAY BE BEAUTIFUL, AND YET..."

This is the lie of the mind,
When fantasy mutates into memory,
Festooned with garlands
And honored by festival days.
As if what was wished for
Were what was.

Freed from natural predators
And fed by false recollection
It roots deep and spreads wide.
Under its now sacred shade
Lie the shriveled seeds of choices
Never made.

PALLIATIVE CARE

That they have all come—
The children she couldn't save—
Must make her wonder
If their ministrations mean
Forgiveness
That she never stood between the dragon
And his wrath,
Though she was always in their corner,
Cowering.

Or does she recognize
In this tearful parade
A familiar charade,
The sustaining fiction
That all was well
In the little world
Of their domestic
Hell.

SPRING

To be sick in spring
Is odious.
The optimism of daffodils
Offends.
The opulence of azaleas
Is a slap in the face.
All those impossible shades of green
A maddening scatter of paint chips
Exhorting renovation
Beyond the resources of mind,
Body, and bank account.

Everywhere
A redundancy of prefix:
Renewal, revival,
Resurrection.

Only the pollen comports
With feeling out of sorts,
Clogging nasal passages
In frank collusion with arterial blockages,
Stinging eyes with familiar tears.

That's the thing about spring:
The sap rises
And the spirit droops
All the more
Because it cannot soar.

MAYBE THIS TIME

Once more with feeling more
Mellow and mature,
Your passion time tempered,
Your memory stocked
With lessons learned,
Satisfied
That neither worry nor weariness
Has tossed you
To his breast.

Perhaps this redo will undo
Past disappointment and make
The cipher of your life
Intelligible: arriving
Back where you started
And knowing each other
For the first time.

BRIEF CANDLE

Burned down to a stub,
Its flame beginning to sputter—
It was then I put out the light,
Not with a blast of breath,
But gently, ceremoniously,
With a shiny silver snuffer.

Why should I not have done it then—
Before the expiring fire smoked the room,
Before guttering wax puddled
On the table?
Why not, since I was able
To keep the end from being
Such a mess?

ALLERGY

Each taste a death
Threat
I dare not but must
Forget
To live.

Everywhere
Friendly fire.
Maximum
Homeland
Insecurity.

What happened
In this green and pleasant land
To turn nurture noxious?
That suddenly I greet
Each gift-bearer as a Greek,
All civilians
Like suicide bombers?

In this downside up,
Outside in,
What does it mean to lose?
To win?
Surrender seems the only way
Even if
Or just because
My white flag makes
A better target.

SUMMER NOW AND THEN

Summer inches in thick
with particulates
and brazen Asian
mosquitoes.
It is a season of sunscreen
and high electric bills.

Once it was a season
of bare feet and
seersucker shorts
bounding in
when school let out,
each day a buffet
of possibility.

It was a season of memory making,
when remembering
was the last thing
on your mind.

HER LAUGH

Her laugh is what her life would be
If only she
Could ride it all the way
Out
Of that fearful place
Her ringing sound is wrung
From,
Heart-heaved, grasping for joy.

Again and again,
Lashed to laughter
She launches herself
From her doomed planet:
And though she never breaks entirely free,
Her persistence shows she knows
Her laugh is what her life should be.

PROTEST

Was he clueless or just careless,
The guy who planted this stinking ginkgo
In my neighborhood—
Who thrust into a perfect row
Of males this female,
Whose fruit every fall
Fouls both the ground and air,
Spreading puke
Everywhere.

Or was it payback
For an underpaying client,
Nature's own time bomb
Set for a future season
When he would be
Long gone.

Or was it rather a deeper instinct of his kind:
The master gardener himself they say
Despoiled his own creation.
It was he who first added the tree,
And the female, and the fruit.
Then came the fall,
And the stench of mortality
Settled over
All.

THE LOVER'S EXCUSE

Forever and a day
Is what we ardent lovers say,
A phrase that's meant to guarantee
Our passion's perpetuity.

It lacks originality
Perhaps, but romantic ecstasy
Demands some such hyperbole.

Forget an Ovid or a Cyrano;
Love's verse garden long ago
Was picked entirely clean. No
Surprises, nothing exotic left.
Without clichés we'd be bereft.

Forgive us, then. For when
The subject is undying love,
Finding something new to say
Would take forever and a day.

TIKTAALIK: OR, IN THE BEGINNING

Was it high or low,
The tide that delivered
The ur-us
To the original shore?

Was there less or more
Deliberation?

Did the withdrawing wave
Leave space and time
To consider:
Here the element we were fluent in,
There terra all incognita.
Did we hesitate, did we linger
On that not yet no man's land—
Then choose adventure?

Or did some careless copies of our protokind
Get caught up in the lifting tide
And tumble to the alien shore,
Dazed among shell shards,
Victimized until
Eventually
Acclimatized?

Perhaps it wasn't either or,
And we came in waves to that virgin shore,
Hopeful and hapless,
Showing even then
The differences to come
Of men.

EXODUS

They stream across sea and land,
the wretched refuse of failed states
and indifferent gods
making claim on the grace
and space of others.
Absolute for life.

Yet foaming butter welcomes only
flour slowly sprinkled
and briskly whisked.
Heaps and handfuls dumped at once
guarantee undigested
lumps.
Not a savory sauce.

So what?
Here they come,
ready or not.

ASHES IN A COOKIE TIN

Biodegradable.
No metal edges.
No plastic surround.
Requirements for burial
In sacred ground.

We will of course comply.
You were always a stickler for rules.

But in the meantime,
In this mean in-between time,
Something more secure,
If not entirely decorous.

Cookies in a tin,
Neatly nestled offerings
In assorted chocolate trim:
A drop, a chip, a sprinkle or a swirl,
German-baked as you were German-bred,
They sweetened last
Your last Christmas.
When you couldn't sing.
When even chocolate
Finally
Lost its taste for you.

So holiday fare becomes funeral wear.
You would approve:
Depression child, original recycler,
No waster of want-nots,
You saved everything,
Even us.

HEARTHSTONE

It used to be pink,
Flesh-toned,
The stone I saved
From the demolition of
Home.

Now it's leached out,
Great white patches spreading
Like some unsightly skin disease.

Maybe the sunlight's too direct.
Or the heater's too close.
Or maybe it was pink only
When the fire warmed it,
When it sat snug in its place,
Part of a whole,
A hearth, a family's beating
Heart.

NEIGHBOR

The house around the corner
—Older even than I—
Empty and emptied waits
For the bulldozer,
Its doom a boon to employment
And the local tax base.

Built to last,
Maintained for eighty years,
Now it sags,
Crossing the threshold back
From home to house,
Its windows blank,
Things growing wild
Around it.

It's ready to give up the ghost,
If houses have ghosts
Like trees their hamadryades
Or bodies souls.
We ought to know
So someone could be there
When they go,
Someone in sacred garb
To sprinkle spelt and salt
In sacrifice,
Or just someone to say thank you
And goodbye.

NAVEL

The autonomy you made
has been repaid by this
pitiful diminution:
from omphalos to belly button,
from true source of the Fountain of Youth
and Apollo's own earth-centering stone,
to a collector of lint and ornament,
occupying prime abdominal
space.

FILL IN THE BLANKS

It used to be easy.
No buried themes to excavate.
Nothing wrestled with or caressed.
Just a simple memory test
With answers by the book—
Something read, something said
Easy to retrieve and place
Snug in its expectant space.

Once a classroom test tossed off
Triumphantly,
Now a diagnostic tool
To mark the march of fool-
ishness:
Blanks thicken into blankness
And filling in is falling in-
to confusion.

AUTO BIOGRAPHY

Our role in the plot thickens
In consistency until it assumes
Predictive power:
A narrative constructing and constricting,
One letter only apart.
Now you're Theseus threading the Theban maze,
Now Gulliver bound on a beach in Lilliput.

One letter only apart: u or i,
I or you.
We are each a tale told by and to,
Impersonations coming true.

TWEAKING CHARLOTTE

To them I am
Adjustable.
I am dosages, settings.
I am waves and beats:
An internal organ they voice
From stops to start and then
Sustain . . .

I am live-wired to measure
The accuracy of their aim.

No going back now for me.
Adjustment must be made
To this remnant of my self
Sufficiency.

So this is my body,
Given up for them
To take apart.

They think that they are working
On my heart.

GOOD FRIDAY

An ordinary day,
When little girls hit high C's
At play, and birds chatter
Unremittingly;
When buds pop, and cars don't stop
For pedestrians.

It is also Good Friday,
A day whose very name
Leads a parade of paradox and puns:
So the son rises by setting,
And the light brightens into darkness
At noon.

It is a day too big for its week,
Its month, its year,
Too big even for this earthly sphere.
Its ambition is cosmic—a stage on which
Only the biggest stars can play.

As if God couldn't die
On an ordinary day.

STEAK DINNER

Did a maiden's stately grace
Lead you to the place of
Sacrifice,
Your horns all gilded and
Beribboned?
Did the pipe and flute salute your coming
There?
Upon your head
Was wine tipped out
And barley scattered round
About?
Did you even give consent
When you bent your head
For the cooling water?
And did a common cry
Go up
When the fatal blow
Came down?

REMEMBERING . . .

my heart leap at your footfall
across my porch—
how expectation whittled down the day
to your sharp knock on my screen door
which opened appetites in me
far more than I had bargained for

or you could satisfy.

JUST FRIENDS

I shipped shoes today
To one who once walked away
From me.
Distance then was interstellar,
All landscapes littoral,
Looking out to sea
For someone lost
To me.

I live literal now,
Where walking wears holes
In soles not hearts
And distance is flat rate
To all parts of a world
Where even loss can be
Insured against.

Every bark is fatal and perfidious
And every voyage ends in shipwreck.
Whether steerage or nearer
My God to thee,
All aboard
Finish as flotsam or fishes.

Yet in the midst
Of the disequilibrating list,
The prow-beaten plunge,
The vertiginous whorl,
Send up a flare:
Not for rescue. Just to mark
That someone, once, was there.

SEA GLASS

Bottles, jars, pieces, shards,
relics of satisfied desire,
now disregarded,
casually discarded

into the sea,
refuse it cannot refuse
to take and then inexorably
remake until

the churning waves return them
to the shore,
more precious now
than anything contained before,
witnessing through the operation of the sea
how beauty comes to be.

GARDENIA

Sweetness unabashed
And unabating,
A gush of too much
You can't get
Enough of:
An olfactory ecstasy
Yoked
To a delicacy so fine
That the merest touch
Defiles,
Curling petals brown
That before were whiter
Than a wedding gown.

Even the end—
The blossom limp against the leaves—
Is a tease of
Contradiction:
Modesty that hangs its head
Or spent passion languishing
On a cool green bed.

"COSI FAN TUTTE"

Obstructed view was all we two
Could afford—
College kids taking our first bite
Out of the Big Apple.
Newcomers to the old Met
We watched lovers fantastically disguised
Test on a dare
The loyalty of their ladies fair.

You couldn't see how much of me
Was in that tale:
Like Ferrando disguised,
Like him breathing in
Your aura amorosa,
But without his script, or song.

So that obstructed view
Was all you ever knew
Of me.

ROMEO

He grew up just enough
To be dangerous
To everyone around him,
Murdering his way through the play
Until at last
His dagger found a home
In the heart
Of Juliet.

She thought because
They made a sonnet together
Their union was meant to last
Forever,
Coupled by a couplet
And sealed with a kiss.
Poor girl,
How could she know
That beneath that party-crasher's mask
Was the face
Of death?

DAVE

No more your words come
Trippingly off your tongue.
The tumor feasting on your brain
Morphs morphemes into sounds
That make sense only
Feelingly.
I see how hard your face works
When your words won't—
Urgent to unload the unsaid
Accumulation of years
Before the train of thought goes on ahead
Without you.

GOT TO

Got to, have to, must—
These are the blessed ones, alive
In the tunnel of their vision,
Accepting indifferently
Whatever if any applause
For how they live
Because

Even they can't say whether
The race is from or to,
Whether sirens call
Or demons pursue.
Aloft
On their single occupancy
Bandwagon
They drive headlong
Over the cliff
Into the promised land.

US

Neither a mismatch nor a perfect fit,
We tried it on
And off, and on and off,
Rhyming the years with cheers and tears.
You're fifty now, more
Than ever dear, and it's finally clear
That all our misfittings were just
The way a glove turned inside out
Would feel on the other hand.

ALL HALLOWS

Silent in echoing churches,
Immobile in glass or stone,
Locked into litanies,
Their virtues utterly
Out of date:
No one knocks at heaven's gate.

On this eve every door opens
Obligingly offering treats
To the insatiable.
Everywhere ghosts and goblins,
Witches and warlocks,
The freaky, the funky, and the infamous
Frolic in the streets
In waves of ages from dusk
To the midnight hour.

Heaven is empty.
Sanctity doesn't sell.
Yet even in our playfulness
We still profess our faith in hell.

THE GRUDGE

Why does my grudge on your behalf
Persist? Why do I insist on hurting
For you, and resist resting
In peace as you are doing
These ten years and more?
Why must I rub this sore?

Those others have died, too, and taken
Their reasons with them: All now
Beyond the reach of reconciliation
Or remorse.
Why not me?

This grudge gives you an afterlife
Preserved in bile—
You whose tenderness of heart
Made so easy to wound and
(Why do I forget?) so quick
To forgive.

FISHING

Moderation comes hard to humankind
Designed for carpe diem—
With eyes bigger than stomachs and
Mouths that bite off more
Than they can chew.
It's easier to grab
Than to eschew.
Eventually we learn
(Through our mistakes, of course,
In no particular order)
That it's the big fish
We should throw back
Into the water.

REGRET

Sins of omission are common enough,
And we readily confess them:
Good deeds slacked, good intentions never acted
Upon.

But it is not the weight of these
That over time
Oppresses the spirit,
Compresses the spine,
And makes us short
As our leftover days.

The undone that undoes us is
The dance
Refused,
The siren song
We stopped our ears against,
The plunge
Conditioned on a toe test.

There are no last rites for a life unlived,
And no final absolution.
For what grace could bend to forgive
Sins of commission
Uncommitted?

BREAK UP

Forgive me that I wound
When I would heal,
That what's meant as balm
Burns. I thought I had
A surgeon's hand and eye,
Keen, deft. Instead I seem
All botch and blunder.

Let's call it quits while
The scale still tips
Toward cherishing.
Yet I know
What I mean as the coup de grace
You'll feel as just another blow.

UNTITLED

Since time has delivered you
from delivering on
the promise of your youth,
make your votive offering now
to the stern god of Ambition:
Hang up your trophies,
your titles and degrees,
and like a long held breath at last
released,
be still, and rest
in peace.

DISFAVOR

What credit do I get
For a favor granted
But begrudged—
Prefaced by a lecture and
Indexed according to its
Inconveniences?

Because from my high horse I saw
A much more sensible course,
And no need for such a need
At all.

Why couldn't I just dismount,
And answer that distress
With a simple, unconditioned
Yes.

DOG WALKING

Short haired and long legged
She stood rigid on the sidewalk
Exposed in all those places
Where his nose inhaled information
Of a most intimate kind.

Only her wild eyes
And a tremor in her thighs
Showed her hair-trigger, knife-edge
Ready—should he presume—
To bolt or bite.

Meanwhile,
The two women chatted
About quotidian things,
The leashes slack in their hands,
All at ease,
Their heads slightly angled
To catch the faint summer breeze.

WATER WORKS

Always the same old question:
What was it like on the beach
That morning in June.
On Omaha beach.
On D-day.

But this time was one time
Too many.
The old man began to bawl.
This veteran
Of the men don't cry generation
Wept as though a reservoir within
Had filled to the brim
And spilled at last
Years
Of unspent tears.

Who is this man,
The children cried.
Where has he been?
And why did he wait so late
To start having
A heart?

THE READINESS IS ALL

I had power to hurt
But did none,
Or little,
Or just some:
Enough to break bonds of connection
Tight beyond chafing.

Unpracticed in such letting go
I didn't know what
To expect:
Surely some recoil at least
From this discharge.

Yet after only days
Apart,
I find some bruising
Of my chest,
But not my heart.

RETAINING WALL

It's leaning now, the old wall,
Yielding to the steady press
Of soil and root and rain,
Giving ground to ground
But not—not yet—
Surrendering.

It's not yet reached its tipping point,
The angle of incline
That will turn decline
Precipitous.

But now its lean is not extreme,
Just a nod, a modest bend
To acknowledge the beginning
Of its end.

MY TRIBE

I need a new tribe,
A shibboleth tribe,
Password defended.

I need a tribe that knows
Hatchets are not for burying
And the smoke of peace pipes is
The plaything of the winds.
A tribe whose dance always begins
With two steps back,
In remembrance
And remonstration.

My tribe will be the chosen ones,
With the wordsword of salvation,
The consonant too high to scale,
Too rough to elide,
Poised at the disarticulating throat
Of the now and forever
Other.

My tribe,
Until that cosmic thrust,
The meteor collision
That will make us all one
Dust.

MAKING THE TEAM

I found an old photo
Of a smiling young boy—
Of me, and I see
I'm wearing the jersey of gold,
Coin of the realm,
Buying entrance.
On a team.

I was fit to fit in,
Suitable to suit up
For the huddle, the handoff,
The sprint down the field,
Exalting
In the bruising embrace
Of brotherhood.

But there was only one season
For the jersey of gold.
Soon urgings unseasonable and strange
Benched me.
Then I played a different game,
And all my running was
For cover.

REVIVAL

So sure, so earnest, and so young—
I surprise myself with him
And begin to believe again:
That this drought-parched, ice-melting
Sea-rising world where
Ignorant armies clash
By night and day
Can be saved.

The assurance of his brain
Bathed in testosterone
Lifts, almost, my lapsed faith
And revives a flicker
Of the visionary gleam.

But is it faith or flattery,
That a man so smart, so young
Would want to recruit someone
Old enough
To be his grandfather?

WRATH

It's a deadly sin,
One of the Big Seven,
So big in fact that even God
Commits it.
But he doesn't die.

I wonder why.

A FISH STORY

I am gutted.
Chipped ice numbs the pain.
My round eye stares
Sightless.

There is still time:
My flesh is fresh,
No odor of decay.
Still time to redeem
The roiling in the net,
The gasp in air,
The steel, the slice, the quick
Evisceration.

There is no consummatum est
Unless you consume:
I need your gut to find
What's left of life
In me.

NON-CANONICAL HOUR

Deep into the midnight hour,
When the book's closed, the tea drunk,
And the bed turned down for sleep,
I wander the house savoring
Stillness.
The streetlights scatter shadows in the room,
And thoughts rise random as bubbles
In a stream, thronging the dark,
Mingling memory and dream.
Then, just then, I want to kneel and pray,
Even though I don't know
What to say
Or who
To say it to.

CANTEMUS

Be always singing.
Sing everything: show tunes and pop tunes
And snatches of arias.
Sing hymns and anthems
And medleys of alma maters.
Sing old songs and new songs
And songs you make up as you go along.
Sing a cappella and accompanied
By every kind of device.
And remember to sing every chorus twice.

Be always singing.
Sing everywhere: in the shower, of course,
And for your supper.
Sing in the street and let the hills
Be alive with the sound of your singing.
Sing when you march into battle
And when you carry the dead home on their shields.
Sing for the sale, and for your promotion.
Most of all, sing to the ones you love.

Be always singing,
Because you never stutter when you sing.

INDEX OF TITLES

A Boy   6
A Fish Story   98
Afterlife   29
Ah   19
All Hallows   83
Allergy   57
"And the great shroud of the sea rolled on..."   75
...and there was light   31
Ann Cobb   42
Anniversary   14
Ashes in a Cookie Tin   64
Auto Biography   69
Azaleas   33

Baseball Season   43
Better Late Than Never   41
Between Rounds   46
Break Up   87
Brief Candle   56

Cantemus   100
Champ   7
"Che gelida manina" 1964   47
"Cosi Fan Tutte"   78
Curtain   51

Dave   80
Disfavor   89
Dog Walking   90

Exodus   63

INDEX OF TITLES

Fill in the Blanks	68
Fishing	85
Gardenia	77
Genesis	30
Gingko Biloba in the Fall	22
Good Friday	71
Got To	81
Hearthstone	65
Her Laugh	59
History	24
Horace	49
Intimations of Mortality	4
Just Desert	20
Just Friends	74
La vie en rose	3
"Leave me, O Love"	40
Lightning Bugs	44
Little Sister	26
Making the Team	95
Maybe This Time	55
Memory	48
"Memory may be beautiful, and yet…"	52
Missing	45
My Tribe	94

INDEX OF TITLES

Navel	67
Neighbor	66
New Year's Eve, 2008	27
Next in Line	28
Non-Canonical Hour	99
Old Men	34
Once	1
Out of His Element	36
Palliative Care	53
Paul	39
Performing for Company	25
Pietà	8
Prometheus	32
Protest	60
Regret	86
Remembering...	73
Retaining Wall	93
Revival	96
Romeo	79
Same Difference	35
Sea Glass	76
Sea Turtle	10
Secret	12
Spring	54
Steak Dinner	72
Storyteller	21
Summer Now and Then	58

INDEX OF TITLES

The Dead	18
The Grudge	84
The Leaf Blower	17
The Lover's Excuse	61
The Old Prayers	9
The Question	38
The Readiness is All	92
The Word	5
Threshold	11
Tiktaalik: Or, In The Beginning	62
Timing is Everything	2
Tweaking Charlotte	70
Two Little Boys	37
Untitled	88
Us	82
Water Works	91
What Have They Done with My Lord?	15
Winter Trees	13
"With how sad steps, O moon, thou climb'st the skies"	16
Wrath	97
Yes	50
Your Messages on the Answering Machine	23

ABOUT THE AUTHOR

Jim Mengert was educated at Princeton (AB) and Yale (PhD), taught English at the University of Mississippi, and then was vice president of a communications consulting firm. Today he works with individual clients such as the Centers for Disease Control and Prevention and teaches courses in Emory University's Lifelong Learning program.